REFLECTIONS

&

JOURNEY TO AN ENDING

Collected Poems

by

Ardath Mayhar

Writing as "Ardath Frances Hurst"

The Borgo Press
An Imprint of Wildside Press LLC

MMVIII

BORGO LAUREATE SERIES
ISSN 1082-3336
NUMBER TWO

FIRST WILDSIDE EDITION

CONTENTS

<u>REFLECTIONS</u>

FOREWORD

When I was three years old, my Dad and I used to sit at the supper table and create long, involved, rhyming narratives, he giving me a line and I giving him a rhyming line.

We dealt with buzzards and grasshoppers and tadpoles and anything else that caught our fancy. By the time I could control a pencil I was writing verse (very childish, of course, but headed in the right direction).

As I grew older and learned my craft, I began marketing my verse to magazines, and over the years I placed dozens in venues as diverse as *The Arizona Quarterly* and *Epos*. These were eventually collected together into two small books of verse.

Journey to an Ending won the publication award offered by South and West at a writers' conference in the Sixties.

Reflections contains work published in a number of different publications, but I put it together myself, using computer, copier, and my own art work. I learned pretty early in the game that you can starve to death quite effectively by trying to make it as a poet.

—Ardath Mayhar
Chireno, Texas
September 2006

JOURNEY TO AN ENDING

RECEIVER

I am honed tender by the years,
each nerve so taut and fine
the subtlest whisper of a star
makes anthems in my ears.

BUZZARD

On an invisible rope of wind,
he balances with ease,
where exhibitionist swallows spin
on a slender breeze.

High above their levity,
cycling like a sun,
in his darkling dignity
answering to none.

In the circuses of the sky,
the buffoons hold their breath
when his sable form drifts by
like the shape of death.

CAT

I am the carnelian cat,
ignoring the passage of time;
for thousands of years I have sat,
stately, rubescent, sublime,
on haunches as supple as stone.

My eyes, old and redder than blood,
have seen aeons break on the world
yet never have blinked as I stood,
my tail geometrically curled,
my spirit aloof and alone.

LASER

This is the rubied eye, whose ardent glance
may pierce a diamond—or a man
and stare through stone and sky.

This beam of reddest power
will, one day, scan through all the air,
sending strange navies to oblivion.

Its naked gaze
will penetrate this planet
with out inquiring probes,

and it will be our messenger to space,
searing outward, arrowed from blind hands,
to pierce the farthest reaches of the sky.

HEPHAESTUS

Hurl your earth-shattering fires,
roar incredible thunders;
ravage forests and fields
with your archaic powers.

We shall hurl bolts of our own;
your inviolate reaches
shake with our lightnings and roar
with the sound of our voices.

Flee to the portals of Zeus!
Still our arts will pursue you!

DESCRIPTION

A body's frail
diameter
holds miracles of might,
compassed in small perimeter,
curiously alight.

And courage is incredible
in such a flimsy frame,
compounded dust, expendable,
dignified with name.

JUNGLE

Here, scarlet pain is crouched,
and gray-winged death must hover,
patient, in the darkness,
seizing as prey those vagrants
who pass the circling fires
into the mortal jungle.

Though watchers be alert
and faithful in their tending,
some must elude their care;
and the waiting beast
will roar and his fangs redden,
and his belly will fill.

Then the quiet vulture,
death the aloof, the patient,
may flap down from his treetop,
ready for the feast.

CORPUS

In this bastion of breath
stalk the armies of life;
there is pain, there is death
in this bastion of breath,
where mortality's stealth
draws a renegade knife;
in this bastion of breath
stalk the armies of life.

HERITAGE

We are filled with fury;
the capacity for violence
is our measure and our curse;
we are animate potentials
of danger and death,
triggered and tense and unaware.

Along the road from beast-hood
we lost the matted hair,
the prognathous jaw,
but we retained an
instantaneous readiness
to kill.

TEMPLE OF DEATH

Upon an ancient hill stand three tall stones;
Their fragile fingers, pointing to the sky,
Still wait, still dream; the shapes that once would
     lie,
Ecstatic, in their angle, left their bones
To bow in gaunt submission to dead gods
Before the altars of antiquity.
An elder race, in strong senility,
Raised its thin columns, flattened the rough clods
To make a place of worship and of death;
Into the place of stones came young and old
To sacrifice their blood and life and breath,
To carpet with their bones the bloody mould;
Now all is crumbled stillness, and the night
Turns slender stones to chilling shapes of fright.

AND WE ARE STILL EVOLVING

The ancients feared the unpropitious skies,
the glaring stars, the savagery of sun;
their fear and their religion met as one
to soothe inimical realities.

Who first, among them, dared to bind a stone
(perhaps a god) into a wooden haft,
and, through the crude efficiency of craft,
proved rock's superiority to bone?

Then one who loathed the mastery of night,
frightened by thunder, lured by a man's brain,
went forth into a world of noise and rain
and filched the fruits of lightning, warmth and light.

And we are still evolving out of fear,
worst of the scourges that have cursed the race,
becoming still and wise, that we may face,
unswayed, all dangers that beset us here.

UNIFIED FIELD

"We are of such stuff as are the stars"—Bethe

> Precise cohesions bind us, star to star,
>   atom to atom;
> propulsions, infinitely circular,
>   limit our freedom.
>
> Electro-magnetism shapes the form
>   of man or planet,
> moves stars on course, powers the under-
>   storm,
>   draws steel to magnet.
>
> Molded and vectored by the self- same
>   forces,
>   man and firmament
> cycle upon their most disparate courses,
>   in swift sacrament.

FORGET THESE EARTHEN WALLS

Forget these earthen walls, this narrow house;
Forget the attic-memories in store;
Abandon it to silence, dust and mouse,
Though its blind windows seek you as before.

Go outward into sun-path, star-dew, time;
Seek in the quietness between the days;
Utter a wordless chanting, as you climb;
Listen to glory, singing through the haze.

There, where the outwardness is all within
And inwardness transcends the finite skies,
Await, in thoughtful space, the aims of men,
And find all purposes behind your eyes.

WITH THE BRIGHT BUBBLES

Let us, felt-footed, seek a way
below the texture of the dark,
go deeper than the interplay
of moonray with a shadow's arc.

Into the depths below a night,
black beyond black, and still and deep,
let us direct our soundless flight,
through the strange hemispheres of sleep.

Leaving our sad, our ageless rest,
we shall explore another place:
deeper than silence, chill as mist,
imperturbable as space.

With the illogic of a dream,
we shall plumb blackest tides of death,
spangling their unaccustomed stream
with the bright bubbles of our breath.

UPON THE VERTICES

Impaled upon the vertices of thought,
skewered upon my own humanity,
an insect, fastened to perplexity,
I am beset by riddles I have wrought.

The earth is made of questions, and the skies,
from the impassioned discipline of law,
give answers that I never may re-draw
into the shapes that we can recognize.

I have implored the dwellers in the deep;
I have besought the very stuff of air,
yet I am left upon my needle, where,
stabbed through with wonder, I can never
      weep.

JOURNEY WITHIN

Come where the nebulae have bled
their milky ichor through the night,
where planetary pilgrims fled
like moths about a star of light.

Come, where the dark is strung with suns,
and clouds of stars rejoice the deep;
where Law is visible, yet runs
with the serenity of sleep.

This universe within a skull
contains more suns than all of space,
forever in a bony hull,
and endlessness behind a face.

PLEA

A waken, wanderer!
The fire-strung paths you walk are winking
     out;
The passioned sparks you sought are cinders,
      now;
Awaken, wanderer!

Open your light-blind eyes!
The fields of flame are flickering and cool;
The hearth of Heaven grays before the night;
Awaken, wanderer!

Awaken, wanderer!
Lest you may walk at last in barren skies
And scuff the ash of Cosmos round your feet,
Awaken, wanderer!

LET US BREAK MOLDS

Let us break molds, smash cages,
freeing young minds from old fetters:
there will be danger perhaps,
terror in all the schools, all the banks,
but lovely fervor.
Let us unmold the pudding-brains,
prettily shaped, and sweetly,
but not for thinking:
let them grow lumpy, as brains should,
and develop bulges.

Truth could be taught in schools!
The ways of reason explained!
Children might even learn to laugh at
                themselves
and at us, but kindly,
and to question our Truths and find their own.
We ran dispense with traditional lies,
such as "learning is fun"
"The Pilgrims came to find religious
        freedom"
"The Civil War began over a question of
        slavery"
and "Arithmetic is easy."

The soft-headed and sloppy-minded trash
which is our daily fare,
"entertainment," if you please,
should be dumped with atomic wastes:
it is more dangerous.

And as for the various bigotries,
prejudices, and assorted cruelties
with which the ignorant carefully
cripple their children's minds—
they may require Divine Fiat.

UNDER OUR SCATTERED EMBLEMS

Under our shattered emblems,
crouching like beasts in pain,
we will recount our errors,
speak of our lost domain.

Then we shall know our blunders,
then we shall see our fault,
faced with the end of glory,
the losers by default.

Each will have been deluded,
cushioned by sated greed,
ignorant of the poison
sapping our failing breed.

Now, by defeat enlightened,
broken in life and breath,
we know, in naked anguish,
we gave ourselves to death.

SPHINX

Why do you crouch, head up, eyes wide,
        listening?
What can you hear, save the mumble of wind,
the dim applause of sand?
Have you heard the soundless melodies
Woven by shuttling atoms?
Have you felt the delicate, interlaced forces,
webbed in your stone frame,
binding you to the universe?
Or do you hear the mindless howl of
        undisciplined ego
rising like a stench from the packed masses of
        men?

Do you feel the bestial aura of jungle,
the miasma of greed-hate-fear that they
        emanate?

Can you discern the rare souls moving,
quietly, quietly, among the ferocious beasts,
building with the clean steel of their spirits?

You have felt the remorseless flowing of time
across your stony haunches.
You have held relentless rivers of men

between your quiet paws.

You have watched the short-lived seasons of
      men,
their puny battles,
which is the reason for the sardonic
      expression
on your frozen lips.

ADVICE TO THE UNDEFEATED

Up from this frozen hour,
rise upon wings of fire,
warming the night with power.
melting the sky with ire.

Leap from this time of slumber.
turn from the realm of death.
spurn all things that encumber
the limbs, the heart, the breath.

Turn from this loss with sorrow,
burn with the future's gain;
blaze through the clouds of morrow
brighter for pride and pain.

LAST DAYS

These are the last days, slipping, bead-on-
      strand,
along the spiral thread of history:
strange, that the mist has lain upon the land
more lovingly.

Never more sweetly has the mist evoked
such leafage and such ecstasies of grass;
never so whitely has the night-mist smoked
where fireflies pass.

Never has Autumn felt so like farewell,
despite the gold and glitter of its light:
we move within a hazed and golden spell
toward what night?

GENESIS

By awful fiat,
God proclaimed the sky:
lesser pronouncement
made the gaseousness
that spawned the suns;
as molten beads,
the planets swirled and swung,
cooling and mellowing,
softening to life.

IN A STILLED INSTANT

In a stilled instant,
I glimpsed the stricken Christ
trapped behind your eyes:
the inarticulate, omnipresent God
born in all of us.

Cradled in curling waters, we began,
the smallest seed
cast in a wondrous sowing;
rising by step and step,
from shape to shape,
a spark of spirit
growing, growing, growing.

Doubting and faulty,
you are sustained, driven,
you are tormented by His divinity,
aflame in human flesh
and frustrated there.

And this, our burning, glorifies our
      dust.

STILL FROM SINAI

Still, from forbidding slopes, rumble Sinaitic
        echoes
and a gray Moses,
erect upon his height,
converses with his God.

The Christus taught a gentler law, but love
is not so stern a staff as fear,
and recalcitrant humanity demands a "THOU
        SHALT NOT,"
a threat of holy wrath.

When will a weary
and undying Moses
be allowed to lay aside his long task
and a matured people go forth
wearing the light yoke
of love?

DEUS EX MACHINA

What precocious godling,
descending from the machine,
gears whizzing, circuits a-buzz,
infallible product of a smug
       technology,
will ease international tensions,
answer all our questions,
feed the hungry?

We are such skilled idolaters,
listening reverently to our own
       creations,
awed by electronics,
dazzled by mechanic tours-de-force,
ready to endow a calculator
with near-divinity
because it adds faster than we can.

Nonetheless,
we will be answered,
we will be succored,
we will be assuaged,
but in God's own way and time.

POINT OF DEPARTURE

Beyond this place
the light grows strange
and seems to race
foreverward.

Beyond this time
of curdled haze,
there is a blaze,
remote and dim,
of afterward.

ENDING

Unclose, my hands, like lilied flowers
      blooming;
prepare to take the penitential nail:
drain this closed heart of harbored mysteries,
through the dark wounds that stain your
      purity.

These that have made the working of my will,
innocent slaves, must suffer now with me,
spiked to the cross of life in martyrdom,
seeking to follow in the way of light.

These open hands, bestarred upon gray wood,
have wrought for good and ill, I am content,
stretched, resting, here upon my being's
      death,
in the dim twilight of a waning world.

40

REFLECTIONS

REFLECTIONS

Through the dark mirror that is history
Shimmer dim motes of human figures, dancing,
Deep in the glass, to their own music, glancing
Through, unconcerned, in their old mystery.
And when the present, preening in the glass,
Meets their despairing gaze, a mortal chill,
A drop of darkness rises up to spill
Like tears from mirrored eyes: We, too, will pass.

The remote images that glint and go
Are all of us; the pirouetting shades,
Depth upon depth, repeat and mock each pose.
Still, slavishly we dip and glide and flow
Step into step through endless glassy glades,
Impotent in our minuet of woes.

NOCTURNE

I hold the night
with such a silver agony
that even stars and shadows
feel my touch.

THE WINDS WILL CHANGE

The winds will change and our lost fleets return
on starry keels, on sails that bow and burn
with splendor drawn from that quiescent deep
where glory rests when spirits turn to sleep;
new gales will bring those ships for which we
      yearn.

No storm may stay them, though the waters churn
and curse at bows; their awful peace will spurn
the turbulence; their shapes, all bright and stern,
will cleave like arrows. Though the waves may leap,
      The winds will change.

There is no power that may overturn
those vessels; only faith may hope to learn
to chart a course when folly's seas are steep.
Across the star-burnt waters they will sweep
to bring a cargo we may surely earn:
      The winds will change.

REQUIEM FOR THE LIVING

I am a long time dying,
but my heart, cross-hatched with scars,
has never flinched from blows.

These wounds
have measured me,
marked my spirit off in inches,
but the cruelest stab
was no unvalued hurt.

I do not retract:
the anguished ways were mine,
and not one instant's agony
would I spare.
I came to peace through pain.

THREE FATES, WORKING

Here Clotho spins amid the fogs of myth,
Draws out a darker strand; her spindle blurs
As it accelerates; its humming purrs
Creative music with no hint of death.
Lachesis smiles as the dark fabric grows
Upon the loom, revealing patternings
In complex webs of interlocking strings
That billow widely as her shuttle slows.

Atropos, watching grimly, clacks her shears;
Another swath is folded, put away;
Somewhere a life is forfeit, spirit fled;
The final arbiter, she holds our fears
Along with that bright steel's decisive play,
Among the strands that are the severed dead.

DRUNKEN OLD WOMAN

You have beheld the Gorgon-face of age
and clasped the wine-jug tighter to your breast,
flung back your head, your laughing face caressed
by the deep prints of laugh and wine and rage
in modeled ridges, like a map of time;
your mouth, a square of suffering and mirth,
shouts sculptured peals to centuries of Earth
and stirs the silent ages with its chime.

From scrawny collarbone your chiton slips;
your buckled knees fling waves of skirt awry;
your arms clasp avidly about a jar
of warm forgetfulness; your stone hand grips
old comfort. Frozen in your destiny,
laugh as you show us as we really are.

THERE IS AN ANCIENT FEAR

There is an ancient fear that walks the night
And makes the skin contract, the spirit quail,
A deep, remembered wariness, a pale
Race-memory of darkness and of fright.
The haunters of the night have ever been
Inimical to those who dwell in day,
So one who walks a darkly shadowed way
Does it with bristling hair: some thing unseen
Walks at his back in silent, stealthy hate,
Chilling his pulse and pounding at his veins;
It waits for some small hastening of gait
To pounce. No intellectual disdains
Can soothe the blood from quick, instinctive fear,
As deeply primal as a Stone Age spear.

SKELETON

There is a beauty in the bones of Man,
Of simple line and stark economy;
Uncluttered bone and angled clarity,
Complete and clean, are our predestined plan.
The architecture of our frame is good,
Inornate and severe: efficiency
Is all its purpose, though its symmetry
In nature-carven bone surpasses wood
Made fair by craftsmen. Chaste simplicity
Is truer loveliness than gaudy art,
But then our quiet, pure, and classic part
Lies unrevealed in death's dark gallery
In naked, unseen beauty, still and white
Beneath the shadow of unending night.

I AM A WARY WARRIOR

Mine is a cautious stance, balanced as a boxer's
against the need for lunge or feint
or evasive footwork;
the old opponent is devious,
quick to catch a lowered guard.

Time was a kindly tutor,
but I learned more stalwart arts
in toe-to-toe matches with life,
slugging and dodging
and panting on the ropes.

Now I am a wary warrior,
somewhat battered
but unafraid of blows.
My foe has hit and hurt;
I know how it feels,
and I can take it.

TIGER IN THE SKULL

Pain snarls
at the bone-walls,
pacing tight circles
in a round room,
glaring through eye-windows
that reflect its furious face.
Each clawed footfall,
electric tail-lash,
subsonic growl
sets the curtaining nerves aquiver
and the trapped tenant
tearing at the door.

MASK

Despair can be
a quiet thing,
a soundless shriek
within the skull;
some eyes bespeak
no damp design
and show no sign.

For pain can be
a buried thing
and hidden deep,
and mouths that, waking, smile
cry out in sleep.

TIME AND A COLD RAIN

Chill Time slips dully
from the eaves,
tracks the shingles,
blunts the edges of the bricks,
pattering its message into our listening souls.

Atom by atom, our structures,
our bodies erode,
slowly, calmly sinking
beneath the long rain
into the cold flood;
and our spirits hear
the molecules wearing away
and each cell sliding
into the narrow rain
down the wet roof
of mortality.

CHILD IN THE NIGHT

Why have you come,
biding me rise
from the supple waters of sleep
in this star-drenched hour of night?

You sway, pale and lost,
between my symbol-hands,
and your eyes still see
the texture of your dream.

What has pursued you
in the fields of slumber,
sending you,
through silver shafts of moon,
weeping, to my door?

MACROCOSM

The warp of space lies
on a weft of time,
and starry shuttles'
bright velocities,
receding swiftly
outward and beyond
scope of thought or lens,
execute their round
compulsive patterns
through webbed galaxies.

TEN-SPEED TRAP

What mad
mechanic spider
dreamed this shape
and spun it
of aluminum and steel
to web a wary
twelve-year heart
into captivity?

THERE IS NO DEEPER VIOLENCE

There is no deeper violence than stone,
No fury like the frozen force of rock,
Flung high, still molten, by some primal shock,
Grown old and hard, defiantly alone.
The incandescence died that it had known,
The continents have cooled, and oceans lock
Their heaving arms about the world and knock
Their foaming heads to bits on sand and stone.

Yet granite cliffs and cairns still war with wind And
tide and sky with ancient arrogance,
Holding their year-worn bodies lean and high.
They are the last of earth to comprehend
True chaos, and their old recalcitrance
Holds up their heads like swords to cleave the sky.

THE EARTH SPOKE

The earth spoke
in voices of thunder and stone;
branches quivered
as the trees slipped sidelong.

We trembled with the hills,
crying aloud
to the old gods
asleep in their high places;
our terror grew
as the land cracked,
swallowing the old women
with the corn they tilled.

The stream ran away into the earth,
and our forest lay broken;
about us was ruin, was death;
we called to all who lived
and weakly they answered,
and we walked away,
carrying babes and firepots,
into the unbroken lands,

CORRIDA OF THE BLOOD

If I were a young bull
in the pride of blackness and fury,

I would go gladly to meet a sword
amid a passion of trumpets
upon a circle of sand.

The old ritual,
virile dance of consummation,
would bear me, pain-proud and snorting,
on crimson veronicas,
leading me from life.

Bulls must die;
not upon a stained block,
beneath a clod's club would I go dumbly,
without protest.

I would go out
upon a blast of rage
in a sear of sun,
pierced cleanly as a warrior,
to die amid bravos and roses.

FIVE GULLS FLYING

Five seagulls going, rowing
through the sky: why
do they wander yonder
as they fly?

What are they seeking, flicking
over   river,
forestland
and meadowland
as if to fly forever?

When will the land again
feel light feet patter?
No matter;
broad wings, white
as ocean light
will home them to the water.

HEAD OF MARCUS AURELIUS

Yours is a cynical face, my friend,
heavy-lidded,
with inward-seeing eyes;
you seem raddled and rent
by labors and frustrations.

You wrestled with an empire,
with barbarians, with your soul:
the empire stood awhile,
the barbarians calmed, in time,
but your spirit, friend Marcus,
still struggles
behind your beleaguered eyes.

MEDITATION UPON MESAS

Built of such blocks as Cheops coveted,
towered and turreted with artfulness,
structures of symmetry and logic stand
untenanted upon this magnitude.

Windowless walls, blind-beautiful facades,
held by their architectured buttresses,
wait, while our culture fumbles into dust,
the long and secret purpose of their time.

What phantom giants
lurk beyond our sight,
longing to know
the cities of the stones?

POTTER'S ENIGMA

There in the shadows
where the winds twist
grit into spirals,
dust into mist,
crumbles a potsherd;
what ceramist,
lost in dim ages,
mosaicist,
shaper of riddles,
enigmatist,
gave it the imprint
of his wet fist?

PALEOLITHIC HORSE

Sheer panic breathes from your fragment head,
stamped into bone by prehistoric fingers.
Your nostrils flare, eye-sockets roll in fright;
a whinny, almost audible, shapes your mouth.

Ears back, mane bristling, you fled:
what Cro-Magnon hunt stampeded you,
heart bursting with your speed?
And who among those hunters
remembered your terror-stricken image
and molded it, living, into history?

A POINT OF LIGHT

In the dark of time,
we stared across blackness
a-snarl with danger
and took comfort
in the distant flicker
that marked another's cave.

Now we know, we feel
our terrible isolation;
in our planet-cave,
we stare across space
at starfire, fearing, hoping that a friend,
a neighbor,
moves in that distant glow.

LAST NIGHT WE TALKED

Last night we talked,
you deep in your chair,
I cross-legged in my rocker,
squaring up the world
with stringent humor
and demanding ethics.

We struck sparks of ideas,
mind to mind
in our old way,
and on a chain of laughter
strung logical ephemera,
gestured into being
by emphatic hands.

Yet below the warmth, the words
lurked an orphaned memory,
dim beneath dream...
why did I ever think
that *you* had died?

I SHOULD HAVE WRITTEN
TO JOHN MASEFIELD

He gave me oceans,
    gulls and whales
        and whipping spray
through all my landlocked life;
he taught me the worth
      of a tall ship,
 and though mine sails no sea
    I steer it
      by a star.

He sang me
    a rover's song
        that held no fear,
and it has comforted
    my heart's
        dark journeyings.

VIEW FROM THE DIVIDE

At the lip of the downward slope,
I stand in sun mellow with westering,
looking across shadow
at rough lands sinking to darkness
and think of the child
who trudged those impossible miles
with only hope and ignorance for guide.

At the edge of the crowning ridge,
I am washed in warmth
as I turn to descend
into the last of living,
walking with steady rhythm
into the sun's eye.

TRAP

Strange shapes have come with muffled steps
Through the surrounding night
to stand before my open door,
Frozen in the light,
While I, in secret solitude,
Laugh low and dip my pen
And chronicle, in many ways,
Things unlike to men.

I set a quiet snare for dreams
And use a subtle bait
And, crouching in a lonely place,
Summon strength to wait.

THE HAUNTED ATTICS

There are hidden places,
The mind's attics,
where old thoughts moulder
and skeletons of dead dreams lie.
Even the grinning bats
and the secret things
that peer from the gloomy corners
are furred with gray dust.

Here are stored
all the fears that make a man:
the crawling darknesses,
the nightmare terrors,
and things more real
and more terrible;
dreadful things
can exist in hidden places,
in the haunted attics.

OUR LADY OF THE FROSTS

She formed like crystal on the icy air,
Shimmered in lacy sparks upon the wind,
Then coalesced, refracting, to extend
Her diamond wings and swirl her jeweled hair.
Frost-flowers blossomed on her silver gown
And etched themselves across her frozen cheek;
Light robed her, as she turned about to seek
Her goal within the dark and shuttered town.

She traced her patterns surely, fingers light
Upon the windows; ice formed where she glanced
And sheathed her pathways; where she went, a
      bright
Track trailed behind her, and cold moonlight
      danced.
Dissolving into dawn, she whirled her cloak
And faded, and a frozen morning broke.

THERE CAME A YEAR

Again the summer winds
walk upon the hills;
orchards swell
with pendant promises;
unstained blue
domes shining days,
and crickets
celebrate in grass...but
there is no music.

Waters laugh among the stones;
no change has come to swallow nest
or birdsong;
colors seem the same, and long winds
walk quietly...
I hear no music.

Night steps quietly,
leaving no frosted footprint;
warmth laps the land in grace...
but there is no music.

DANCER

The black dancer,
spotlighted in moonglow,
rises on dark toes
and ripples into the air;
a descending whirl
blurs his satiny shape,
turning it into a rag of darkness,
ripped from the night.
His agile body is distilled
of grace and strength,
and his golden eyes
hold all the moons
of eternity.

DRAGONFLY

Needled azure,
standing in the air,
is hung from wings
of pale lace,
vibrantly invisible.

It stitches swift patterns,
subtle chains,
bright loops
upon the simple fabric
of the air.

TEMPLE

I go to God
through cathedralled trees
and the painted windows
of the wind.

THE SILVER CATTLE OF THE SEAS

The silver cattle of the seas
graze deep in salty fields,
seeking through drifts of magic trees
the fodder Ocean yields.

The nervous herds flash, luminous,
about their ancient place,
for all their world is perilous
to all their shining race.

The darkling wolves that prowl the deep
hunt in a wavering wood
to slaughter heedlessness and sleep
and taint the ways with blood.

NOW I HAVE SEEN A SWALLOW

I never saw a swallow
until my years were long
and I had taught my ardent heart
a still and sober song.

Long years my heart lay fallow;
I never thought to be
caught up, flung laughing on the wind
in that old ecstasy.

Now I have seen a swallow
go dancing in the air
and cannot still the soaring self
that wills to join her there.

DISPLACED PERSON (I)

We moved in long slow cycles
with tide and sun, season and year,
orbiting in calm, in certitude, among
labors dictated by animals and earth,
free of little wants and fears.

Our hands moved in deep soil,
eyes knew suffering and stars;
we knew the taste of salt sweat,
the good weariness of muscle and bone.

We lived strongly in a stringent Eden,
but now, cast out by change,
we cycle secretly inside our hearts,
crumble dirt in frustrated hands,
cultivating a hidden seed of hope.

I, LIKE FIRE

I,
like fire
require
things I do not require
but need to feed
the flame
that burns beneath my name.

I live upon the earth,
a blaze upon the hearth,
consuming, bone and blood,
an elemental brood.

I,
like fire,
expire
with passion and with ire,
to find
behind
my spark
smoke-kingdoms in the dark.

END OF A SONG

East of sun, west of moon
I may wander no more,
for the young, witching tune,
east of sun, west of moon,
that is silenced too soon
seldom pipes as before:
east of sun, west of moon
I may wander no more.

KITE FLYING DAY

This is a day that makes me want a kite—
The gusting wind would take it from my hand
And hurl it up, would test the straining strand,
Buffet the brittle shape against the bright
March sky. The wind would stream about my face,
Push at my back while sunbeams warmed my bones
And new grass, springing deep among the stones,
Crushed by my sandaled feet, perfumed my race.

Now I am weary, stiff in hands and knees,
But I remember secrets of the sky
I learned among the sorceries of spring:
For I have flown my spirit on a breeze,
Looked down upon the world from eagle-high,
While soaring on a wood and paper wing!

OUT OF THE BURNING DAYS

There in the willow trees,
covered in rue,
let me find comforting
shelter in dew!
Shadow me! Shadow me,
safe from the sun,
down in the root-havens
where the ants run.

Deep where the grasshoppers
fiddle their lays
let me lay down my bones;
through quiet days
all the small people will
render a part,
send me to dust again
with a cool heart.

WEB OF AUTUMN

This weave of autumn is a warp of gold:
Embroidered geese in geometric skeins
And bright-dyed forests decorate the old
Time-haunted tapestry. The cobweb stains
Of age may cloud it with nostalgic bloom
And dust of other years may dim its face,
But when it hangs in an October room,
Its glow may warm the chill from any space.

There hangs the last of summer's burning blue;
Our bones can feel the creeping in of chill;
Behind our eyes, the rain's beginning, too,
Though this embellished glory wraps us still,
And we are held in an ensorcelled weft
To gaze down autumns we have lived and left.

A COLD AND SLANTING RAIN

Hard on the heels of autumn's dreamy haze
there comes the first of winter's silver rains
to shrivel all our spirits; amber days
turn chill and gray, and all the weathervanes
swivel to northward. Now we fasten doors
and shut our windows to the elements;
we feel a closing in, as winter roars
among the year's fast-fading cerements.

The generosity that summer knows
is damped to embers inside winter walls.
The hearthfire spits and sings; the cold wind blows
beyond our rooms. We do not hear the calls
of those locked out to face the stormy night
outside our circle and beyond our sight.

THE FOREST WAITS

The forest waits, but I cannot return,
with round-eyed wonder, to the deeps of fern,
the root-clenched havens that I used to know.
My heart has lost the newly minted glow
that woke there in the tree-lanes long ago.

The years have changed the child that used to yearn
to meld into the lichen or to burn
with leaf-fires, spring and autumn, and to learn
the wood-lore of the snail. Though I may go,
          The forest waits.

Another being now I can discern
in mirror-pools: this one can never earn
old recognitions, for time's quiet flow
has sundered self from self, and I must grow
to meet the perils of adult concern.
          The forest waits.

DISPLACED PERSON (II)

Up from ageless oceans, crawling,
came a stubborn spark of life,
growing, learning to change and to conquer,
to creep—eventually to run.

I m a child of ocean, of the thundered sea,
the tortured surf, the moon-enslaved tides,
a salt-blooded creature, stranded,
surrounded, lost in forested hills.

Amoebic ancestors lift voices in my blood,
weeping salt tears for our cradle,
the passionate, green-breasted mother,
who is lost to our orphaned race.

SKYFARERS

Beyond the silver boundaries of earth
lie midnight oceans, on whose tenuous waves
the planets plow immense Great Circle routes:
ships passing in the distance cannot hail
across those gulfs to share a mutual need
or greeting. Though we long to cross the space
between, no craft has journeyed there, as yet.

We build great vessels chained by gravity
and think that one day we may loose their ties
and send them reeling into the beyond.
Our pilot-vessels search beyond our gaze
for other farers crossing that great void,
to find a brother race among the stars.

STAR CHART ON EYELID

Lie quietly:
     delineate the intricate maze,
     the bright-hot paths of pain;
     see the light-traced map
     drawn inwardly,
     stabbed with stars of anguish
     where mortality passes.

Lie quietly:
     Upon insides of eyelids
     project astronomers' charts
     of systems and galaxies,
     envision magnetic fields
     gemmed with suns'
     interlocking orbits.

Lie quietly:
     Overlay the shining patterns
     with a starry web of pain.

NOTE TO DR. DEBAKEY

Build me a heart of plastic and of steel,
replacing this too-vulnerable thing
that struggles in its bone-cage, clamoring
to the cold brain, "Resemble me and feel
my sorrow for the suffering. Anneal
your thoughts to pain and problems." Shuddering,
I slam protecting doors between; their ring
echoes in tender membranes not of steel.

These are grim days of pain and perfidy,
revising in their ultra-modern fields
brutality's old horrors and black arts.
I am beset, and my necessity
requires an armorer to forge new shields,
to make (oh why?) a metal-fashioned heart.

TERMAGANT'S TONGUE

She honed her voice on bitterness and wrath,
sharpened it raw to pierce unwary ears,
and wielded it from lips that greed had shaped,
self-pity's taste had soured.

Her railing was a blade: no child but flinched
to feel it carve the runnels of his heart
or know its knifing, even through his sleep,
to sever him from dream.

Now she looks down to death; in misery
and growing fear, she hunts her threadbare soul,
mends it, shakes out the dust, but never tries
to dull her dagger tongue.

VISION THROUGH A GLASS

Through the icicle lens
of dispassionate intellect
the blurred blueprint sharpens;
illegible characters clear;
the shape of living becomes simple
white lines against the dark.

Then the clothing of brute beast
raises its hackles,
shakes its hide,
shivering the cold pane of reason
into splinters.

The pattern dims
in a mist of hot breath;
the lines are lost
in a blur of animal emotion.

WHISPERS

Perhaps the wind blows harder
through the leaves beyond this wall;
there are whispers there
not formed by human lips,
shaping syllables
that chill the listener
with unremembered meanings.

Do great moths flutter
dark wings against the stones
or lizards slither,
minute scales rasping softly?
It might be serpents,
twining in reptilian ecstasy;
do not say that those are words!
Any who might utter them
Are old dust,
layered in brick tombs.

Listen! Listen!
I shut my ears with frantic fingers
and hurry along overgrown paths
toward a distant light.

MEMORY IN MIST

It is so still;
misty waters,
moving in silken furrows,
whisper, whisper,
as the interjections of gulls
puncture the grayness.

Listening,
I breathe salt-velvet
into wet lungs,
cloak my wanderings in fog
and quiet,
but I remember...

clash of shattered waters
against rock,
gnashing of stony teeth
of ship's timbers,
cries, not of gulls,
here where the mist thickens.

KILLDEER

Why does the killdeer
circle the night,
crying without pause or rest
through moon-shot darkness,
its lament wheeling, wheeling
about me?

Sitting in a dew-damp chair,
beneath a red moon waning,
I cannot go quietly to my bed;
my agony nails me here,
as stars curve westward
and the bird cries,
and instinct calls,
"My son! My son! My son!"

No answer comes to straining ears;
only the killdeer's plaintive cry
slices the night
into curves of pain,
and my son does not return.

VIEW OF TOLEDO, EL GRECO

This nightmare city
clings to heaving hills
beneath a sky
of terrible shadow
and fearful light;
the lonely buildings jut,
defenseless,
between earth and heaven.

Somewhere within,
souls convinced of doom and
        damnation
huddle in prayer,
tombed with a nameless guilt,
awaiting a frightful judgment
that never comes.

SHAPER OF WORDS

Recalcitrant slabs of language
yield to the hammer of feeling
and the chisel of art, shaping,
stony and reluctant, into images of
      thought.

The sweating sculptor,
      no effete and flimsy poet,
braces himself against the laws of
      physics,
the habits of spirit, prayerfully
      chipping away
the ugly, the evil, the cruel.

Passion can permeate marble words,
shape obdurate concepts
into towering figures
with the look of truth.

GRECIAN RACEHORSE, 485 BC

Prouder in parian whiteness
than your kind
has ever been, you whinny,
stepping forth on delicate
marble hooves,
neck arched,
nostrils wide to snort,
ready for the blood and dust,
the pounding excitement
of a long-forgotten race.

CALLIGRAPHIC COMMENTARY

A half-century ago, I took a pencil
into my small square hand
to form letters, words, sentences,
opening a door
into worlds of delight.

Habit and training shaped slanting script
that could resemble a picket fence
in a windstorm, or, at its best,
a genteel copperplate
of deceptive decorum.

With sudden decision, I changed
to a clean and easy script
that flows from my hand effortlessly:
minute brain-changes
recharged, renewed me.

Hand and head mesh so closely
it is hard to divide cause from effect;
while mind indisputably directs the hand,
I have proved to myself
that the system is also a closed loop.

I REMEMBER JUNE

When November's damp warps my bones,
and chill wind tatters my edges,
I remember that warm vigor
driving through my youth,
urging me to attack
work beyond my strength and size.

Hayfield summers tempered me;
winters of ice-coated bales
damaged joints, numbed hands,
set in place the arthritic ambush
that waited down the years
to pounce.

Old age is a state of bones,
but mine were used to their limits
before falling into decay;
none of my pain is regret—
warm surges of satisfaction
counter the cold aches.

CRY LONE

Chill wind harps gray stone;
gray waves crash;
and riding the wrack, a lone gull
faces the sea,
treading air,
guarding bleak shores
from storm.

Wind cries over cairns;
spray and sand
write intangible, bitter things
as waves slide between rocks,
scrawling
upon the foam-flecked beach
unreadable hieroglyphs.

Cry lone
across gray sky,
heaving waters,
wounding wind,
a staunch and single gull.

FROM THE MISTS OF SPRING

Out of the greening mists of young leaves
and hawthorn bloom and evening primrose,
into the busy turmoil of life,
there churned a black wind,
dank with threat.

We who had breathed the scented air
turned cold, our stomachs knotted
with impending loss;
death brushed us all with dark wings,
breathed fear into our hearts.

Fearing, we hoped.
Hoping, we persevered,
helpless yet intent upon our goal.
This time we have prevailed…perhaps;
this time the worst did not happen,
but now we wait for another wind
that will sweep our world away.

FOX IN DAWNLIGHT

Walking upon your way,
neat-footed in dew,
you raised your head;
I stood above
in gray dawnlight
and met your golden gaze.

Misted space lay between, but we looked,
eye into eye,
for a stilled moment;
then *you* flickered into fog,
and I went forward
seeing, for a time,
through golden eyes.

THOUGH NOT A DRYAD

Inside, I am a forest;
hickories loom, pines whisper, elms and
    sweetgums
rustle their secret songs
to the interior ear
that listens always for leaves in wind.

A childhood spent wandering
over wooded hills that peered out
toward distant horizons,
through gentle valleys, hiding
secret streams in their depths,
where minnows and crawfish
attended to their esoteric businesses,
marked me indelibly.

Confined to pavements,
stacked dwellings filled with people
who know nothing of terrapins or katydids,
I wither, and not slowly;
such imprisonment
is like a zoo to a tiger
or a pen to a wild horse,
a thing of horror and dread.

I will go free among the trees,
no matter if my limbs grow stiff
and my breath short;
I will limp away, when my time comes,
into an autumn wood.

A CELEBRATION OF FORESTS

The way to the woods
lay up close-cropped pastureland
that was starred with bluets,
cross-hatched with cow trails;
this was a hill made for running up,
arms wide on wind
as if to leap into the crowning blue.

A green heaven lay on the other side,
with a rut-track twisting down
past infant sweetgums,
beneath squirrel-proud oaks and hickories,
under pines
that sang of rushing air.

There was a great rock set in a glade,
where I could sit, scarcely breathing,
to watch jays quarreling
over old acorns,
a newly varnished terrapin
bulldozing his determined way,
or, frozen in bone-chill,
a coachwhip, snaking
on his dark and leaf-rustling path.

Downhill through new green

106

in the scent of young leaves,
blackhaw, and huckleberry bloom,
the path wriggled, leading feet
past a plague-wracked hickory,
whose very shape was fear,
into close-woven tunnels of elm and hawthorn,
where milkweed blossomed
and jack-in-the-pulpit
drew bare knees to damp earth,
small hands to lift hanging hoods.

At road's end, a pond
held a small sky in its cup,
with perch and minnows,
cottonmouth moccasins and yellow-vested
bullfrogs in green tights,
which would leap with startled yelps
and belly-flop to safety.

There I could sit
in a shaded borderland between
sun-shimmered hayfield and dim forest,
savoring both,
with an unpocketed book for lagniappe,
among nesting cardinals
and chimney-building crawfish,
surrounded by peace
and the world's wonder.

DOWN THE LONG DAYS

FOR MY FATHER

You are not here
as a separate physical presence;
your face has gone onto otherwhere,
but a part of you
pumps steadily through my arteries.

My hand is a miniature
of your square one,
with a little of your skill, your gentleness,
a touch of your warmth
and steadfastness.

Inside my skull
there are recorded years
of quiet words and ways,
laughter,
exploding novae of ideas
and tempers.

REFLECTIONS; JOURNEY TO AN ENDING, BY ARDATH MAYHAR

So long as I endure,
you will be with me,
and we will go
down the long days together
in the blood and bones
of my sons.

INTO THE FOG-PATH

The leaves hush underfoot,
and the low mist fingers
the forest, gently stilling
rustle to whisper to quiet.

Steps die into stillness;
words quiver, unspoken,
behind fogged lips.

In the dim aisles, motion
is fluid, holding no emphasis,
no urgency, no living need;
ultimate compulsion drives me
down through the wet wood
toward waiting darkness,
deep into final silence.

MEMENTO MORI

If you look upon my dead face,
in time to come,
imagine these stone lips folded
to hide a wicked grin;
arranged precisely in pious attitudes,
these hands will miss
their unorthodox tasks.

Feet, frozen in used-up clay,
will long to run
up grassy slopes
or to pick their way amid tangles
and overgrown paths
in forests now forgotten.

If, against my wishes,
some man of the cloth
mouths platitudes,
if anything is left of myself
it will be protesting silently;
do not be surprised
if you hear thunder.

ACKNOWLEDGMENTS

"Description" and "Upon the Vertices" were published in *Epos*.

"With the Bright Bubbles" was published in *Epos* and the *Epos Anthology*, 1964.

"Unified Fields" was published in *Voices*, May-August, 1962.

"Buzzard" was published in *Prairie Poets*.

"Let Us Break Bones" was published in *Flame*.

"Temple of Death" was published in *Arizona Quarterly*, 1950.

"Sphinx" was published in *Flame*, 1962.

"Reflections" was published in *International Who's Who in Poetry Anthology 1972*.

"Nocturne" was published in *Quicksilver*, 1954.

"The Winds Will Change" was published in *Deep South Writers and Artists Annual, 1976-77*.

"Requiem for the Living" was published in *Peopled Parables: New York Forum Anthology*, 1975.

"Three Fates, Working," was published in *The Lyric*, 1988.

"Drunken Old Woman" was published in *South and West*, Spring, 1968.

"There Is an Ancient Fear" was published in *Kaleidograph*, 1952.

"Skeleton" was published in *The American Bard*, 1952.

"I Am a Wary Warrior" was published in *The Archer*, 1977.

"Tiger in the Skull" was published in *Cardinal Poetry Quarterly*, February/March, 1972.

"Mask" was published in *Poetry Dial*, 1966.

"Time and a Cold Rain" was published in *American Bard*, 1970.

"Child in the Night" was published in *Oregonian Verse*, The Portland Oregonian, 1971.

"Macrocosm" was published in *Quoin*, 1974.

"Ten-Speed Trap" was published in *Encore*, 1975.

"There Is No Deeper Violence" was published in

Arizona Quarterly.

"The Earth Spoke" was published in *Texas Quarterly*.

"Corrida of the Blood" was published in *Oregonian Verse*, Portland Oregonian, 1976.

"Five Gulls Flying" was published in *American Bard*, 1969.

"Head of Marcus Aurelius" was published in *Mark Twain Journal*, 1968.

"Meditation Upon Mesas" was published in *Encore.*

"Potter's Enigma" was published in *CycloFlame*, March, 1974.

"Paleolithic Horse" was published in *Oregonian Verse*, The Portland Oregonian, 1970.

"A Point of Light" was published in *CycloFlame*, 1970.

"Last Night We Talked" was published in *The Archer*, 1977.

"I Should Have Written to John Masefield" was published in *American Poetry Association Anthology*, 1982.

"View from the Divide" was published in *Voices International*, 1973.

"Trap" was published in *Oregonian Verse*, The Portland Oregonian, 1968.

"The Haunted Attics" was published in *United Poets Magazine*, 1955.

"Our Lady of the Frosts" was published in *Pandora*, 1988.

"There Came a Year" was published in *Oregonian Verse*, The Portland Oregonian, 1976.

"Dancer" was published in *Bitterroot*, 1972.

"Dragonfly" was published in *American Poet*, 1968.

"Temple" was published in *American Poet Magazine*, 1955.

"The Silver Cattle of the Seas" was published in *Kaleidograph*, 1955.

"Now I Have Seen a Swallow" was published in *Driftwood East*, 1975.

"Displaced Person" was published in *Oregonian Verse*, The Portland Oregonian, 1972.

"I, Like Fire" was published in *Cyclotron*, 1965.

"End of a Song" was published in *CycloFlame*, 1973.

"Kite Flying Day" was published in *The Lyric*, 1989.

"Out of the Burning Days" was published in *Driftwood East*, 1975.

"Web of Autumn" was published in *The Lyric*, 1988, and reprinted in *Anthology of Magazine Verse, 1989-90*.

"A Cold and Slanting Rain" was published in *The Lyric*, 1989.

"The Forest Waits" was published in *Writer's Journal*, 1993.

"Displaced Person" was published in *Oregonian Verse*, The Portland Oregonian, 1973.

"Termagant's Tongue" was published in *CycloFlame*, 1971.

"Vision Through a Glass" was published in *Yearbook of Modern Poetry 1971*.

"View of Toledo, El Greco" was published in *Cardinal Poetry Quarterly*, 1972.

"Shaper of Words" was published in *Major Poets*, 1976.

"Grecian Racehorse, 485 BC" was published in *Oregonian Verse*, The Portland Oregonian, 1969.

TITLE INDEX

ABOUT THE AUTHOR

The author of sixty-two books, more than forty of them published commercially, **ARDATH MAYHAR** began her career in the early eighties with science fiction novels from Doubleday and TSR. Atheneum published several of her young adult and children's novels. Changing focus, she wrote westerns (as **Frank Cannon**) and mountain man novels (as **John Killdeer**). Four prehistoric Indian books under her own name came out from Berkley. Historical western *High Mountain Winter* was published by Berkley Books under the byline **Frances Hurst**.

Recently she has been working with on-line publishers. *A Road of Stars* was her first original novel to appear in print-on-demand format. Many of her out-of-print titles are now available from e-publishers fictionwise.com and renebooks.com; other OP novels are soon to be reprinted via Wildside Press and Amazon.com.

Now in her seventies, Mayhar was widowed in 1999, after forty-one years of marriage, and has four grown sons. The bookshop she ran with her husband for fifteen years was closed after his death. She now works at home, writing short fiction and nonfiction, and doing book doctoring professionally. Her web pages can be found at:

w2.netdot.com/ardathm/
and
http://ofearna.us/books/mayhar.html